D0246764

Whales and Dolphins

KINGFISHER

Kingfisher Publications Plc
New Penderel House
283–288 High Holborn
London WC1V 7HZ
www.kingfisherpub.com

First published by Kingfisher Publications Plc 2005
4 6 8 10 9 7 5 3
3TR/0106/PROSP/RNB(RNB)/140MA/F

Copyright © Kingfisher Publications Plc 2005

All rights reserved. No part of this publication may be reproduced,
stored in a retrieval system or transmitted by any means, electronic, mechanical,
photocopying or otherwise, without prior permission of the publisher.

A CIP catalogue record for this book is available from the British Library.

ISBN-13: 978 0 7534 1069 1
ISBN-10: 0 7534 1069 9

Senior editor: Carron Brown
Designer: Joanne Brown
Cover designer: Poppy Jenkins
Picture manager: Cee Weston-Baker
DTP co-ordinator: Carsten Lorenz
Artwork archivist: Wendy Allison
Production controller: Jessamy Oldfield

Printed in China

Acknowledgements
The publishers would like to thank the following for permission to reproduce their material. Every care has been taken
to trace copyright holders. However, if there have been unintentional omissions or failure to trace copyright holders,
we apologise and will, if informed, endeavour to make corrections in any future edition.
b = bottom, *c* = centre, *l* = left, *t* = top, *r* = right

Photographs: *cover* Seapics/Doug Perrine; 1 Seapics/Masa Ushioda; 2–3 Getty/Taxi; 4–5 Nature pl/Brandon Cole; 6 Minden/Flip Nicklin;
7*t* Seapics/Armin Maywald; 7*b* Seapics/Doug Perrine; 8–9 Seapics/Doug Perrine; 8*b* Nature pl/Sue Flood; 9*b* Seapics/Ingrid Visser;
10 Minden/Flip Nicklin; 11*t* Seapics/David B Fleetham; 11*c* Seapics/Mark Conlin; 11*b* OSF/David Fleetham; 12*b* Seapics/Michael S Nolan;
13*t* Minden/Mitsuaki Iwago; 14–15 Corbis/Craig Tuttle; 15*t* Seapics/Doug Perrine; 15*r* Corbis/Lester V Bergman; 15*b* Seapics/Doug Perrine;
16–17 Alamy; 17*t* Seapics/Hiroya Minakuchi; 17*b* Seapics/Masa Ushioda; 18–19 Seapics/Duncan Murrell; 19*t* Seapics/Philip Colla;
20–21 Minden/Flip Nicklin; 20*b* Ardea; 22–23 SeaQuest; 23*b* Seapics; 24–25 Minden Flip Nicklin; 25*t* Seapics/Masa Ushioda;
25*b* Seapics Xavier Safont; 26*b* Seapics Hiroya Minakuchi; 26–27 Seapics Masa Ushioda; 27*t* Seapics Robert L Pitman;
28*b* Seapics/James D Watt; 29*t* Seapics/Bob Cranston; 30–31 Seapics/Doug Perrine; 31*t* Seapics/James D Watt;
31*b* Seapics/Masa Ushioda; 32–33 Seapic; 32*b* Seapics/Hiroya Minakuchi; 33*t* Seapics/John KB Ford; 34 Minden/Flip Nicklin;
35*t* Corbis; 35*b* AA; 36–37 SeaQuest; 36*c* Corbis/Peter Turnley; 38–39 Seapics/Phillip Colla; 39*t* Minden/Flip Nicklin;
39*b* Minden/Flip Nicklin; 40–41 Minden/Mike Parry; 41 Corbis; 49 Minden/Flip Nicklin.

Illustrations: 12–13 Michael Langham Rowe; 23*t*, 28–29 Steve Weston
Commissioned photography on pages 42–47 by Andy Crawford. Project-maker and photoshoot co-ordinator: Miranda Kennedy
Thank you to models Lewis Manu, Adam Dyer and Rebecca Roper

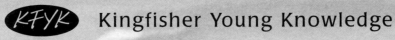

KFYK Kingfisher Young Knowledge

Whales and Dolphins

Caroline Harris

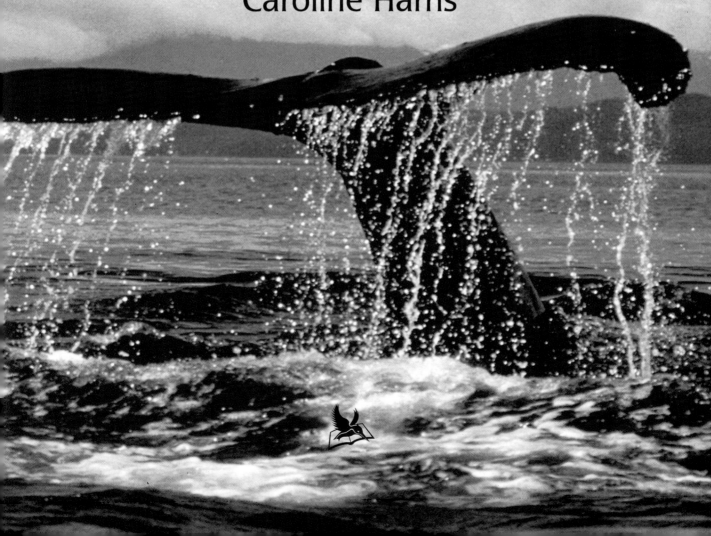

Contents

What are whales and dolphins?

Whales and dolphins are mammals that live in water. They have warm blood and swim to the ocean's surface to breathe.

Baby care

A dolphin mother usually gives birth to one baby at a time, called a calf. The newborn calf swims close to its mother's side for the first few weeks.

mammals – warm-blooded animals that feed their young on milk

Bristly faces

Most mammals are covered with hair or fur. This porpoise's skin is smooth, but young cetaceans and some adults still have hairs on their faces.

Grand old age

Dolphins can live up to 50 years old, while large whales such as this southern right whale may live to be 100!

cetaceans (said 'si-tay-shiens') — group name for whales, dolphins and porpoises

All around the world

There are more than 80 types of whale, dolphin and porpoise. They live all over the world – in freezing oceans, tropical seas and even in rivers.

Icy white

The beluga is also called the white whale. It makes its home in the very cold Arctic seas around Canada, Alaska and Russia.

tropical – a hot, dry area near the Equator

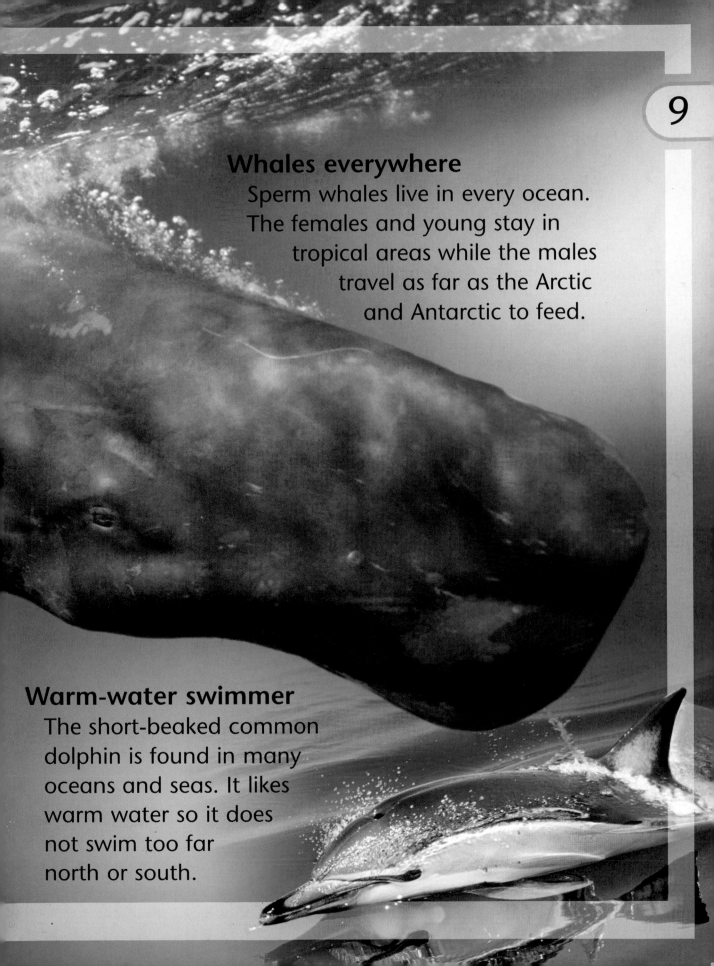

Whales everywhere
Sperm whales live in every ocean. The females and young stay in tropical areas while the males travel as far as the Arctic and Antarctic to feed.

Warm-water swimmer
The short-beaked common dolphin is found in many oceans and seas. It likes warm water so it does not swim too far north or south.

Amazing creatures

Whales and dolphins come in some incredible shapes and sizes. Did you know that the largest animal on earth is a whale?

Dolphin magic

The boto, or Amazon river dolphin, is one of four species of dolphin that are found only in rivers. It is also called the pink dolphin because it has rose-coloured skin.

species – a set of animals or plants with the same features

Sea giant

The blue whale is the world's largest mammal. It can weigh 190 tonnes – the same as 32 elephants. A blue whale this huge has a heart the size of a car!

blue whale

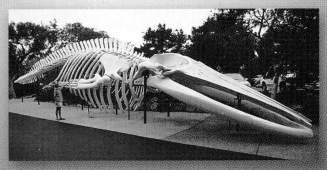

skeleton of a blue whale

Water unicorn

The male narwhal has a tusk that can reach three metres long. Tales of unicorns may have begun when people first saw narwhal tusks.

unicorn – *mythical animal like a horse with a long horn*

Ancient
whales

When the dinosaurs died out, mammals began to live in many different places. This is how whales and dolphins came to live in the oceans.

Digging up the past

We know about ancient cetaceans through the fossils and bones they left behind, such as this dolphin skull.

fossils – any evidence of living things from the past

Grass-eating cousins

Cows, sheep, whales
and dolphins share
the same ancestor –
an ancient mammal
that lived on land
and ate leaves.

Early whale

Basilosaurus lived
40 million years ago. Over
a long time, the land mammals
that moved into the sea changed
their shape to suit life in the water.

ancestor – an animal from which later animals have developed

Built for the sea

The smooth, long shape of cetaceans means they are able to swim through water easily. Salty seawater is good at keeping heavy things buoyant, which is why whales can grow very large.

Full power

Instead of back legs, cetaceans have immensely strong tails with two flat paddles called flukes. Bottlenose dolphins can stand up using their tails alone.

buoyant – *able to float in the water*

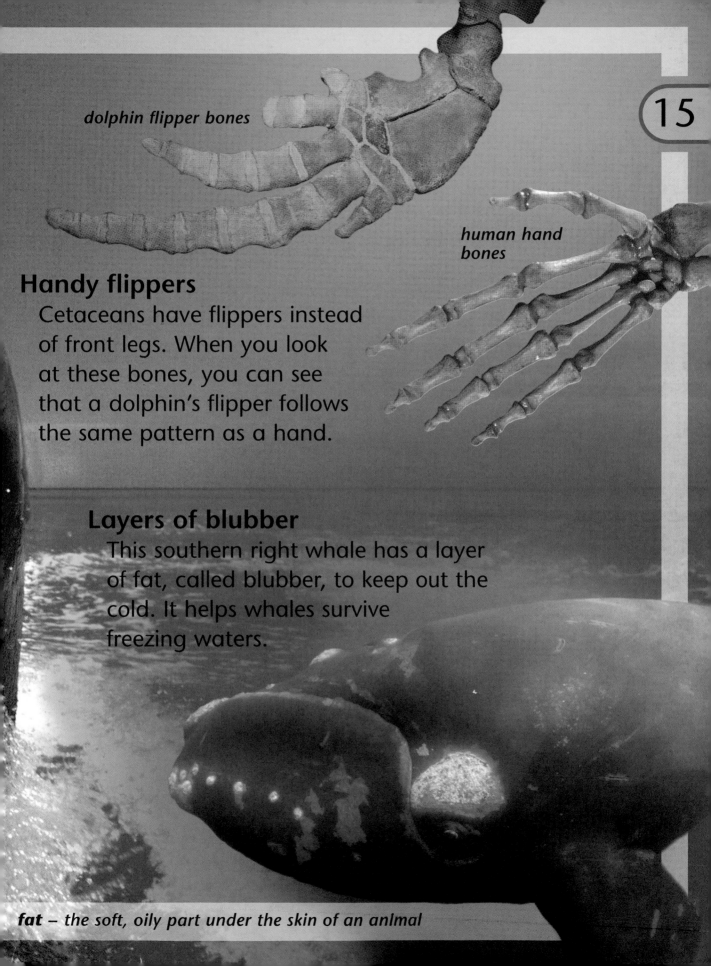

dolphin flipper bones

human hand bones

Handy flippers

Cetaceans have flippers instead of front legs. When you look at these bones, you can see that a dolphin's flipper follows the same pattern as a hand.

Layers of blubber

This southern right whale has a layer of fat, called blubber, to keep out the cold. It helps whales survive freezing waters.

fat – the soft, oily part under the skin of an animal

Coming up for air

Like other mammals, whales and dolphins breathe using their lungs. This means coming to the surface to take in fresh air and blow out used air.

Deep down
Most whales can stay underwater for half an hour before needing to take a breath. Cetaceans take in air through a blowhole in the top of their head.

lungs – the parts inside the body used for breathing

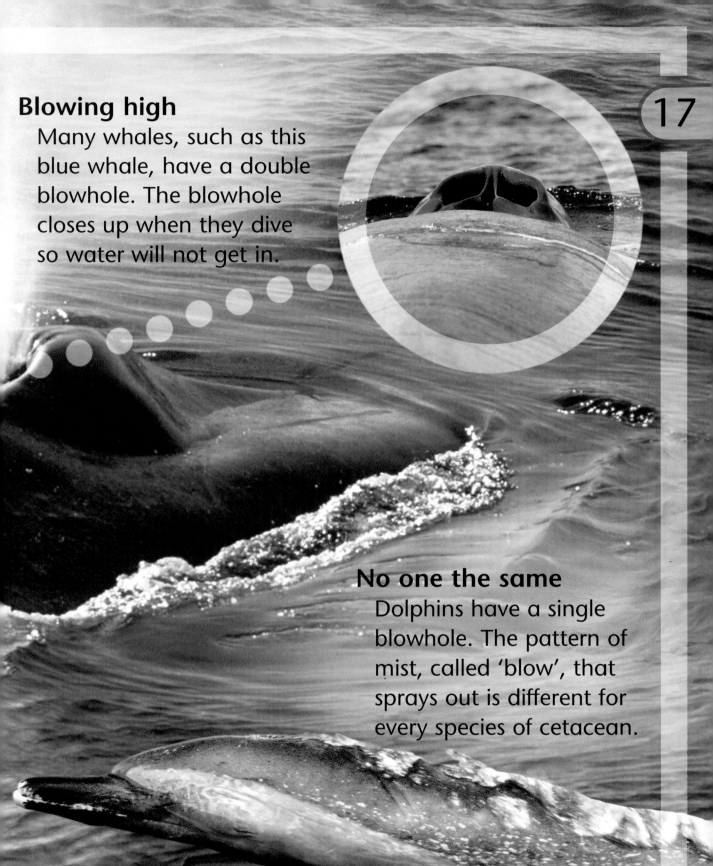

Blowing high

Many whales, such as this blue whale, have a double blowhole. The blowhole closes up when they dive so water will not get in.

No one the same

Dolphins have a single blowhole. The pattern of mist, called 'blow', that sprays out is different for every species of cetacean.

blowhole – the airway that whales, dolphins and porpoises breathe through

Filter feeders

Cetaceans are split into two groups: those that have teeth and those that do not. The toothless whales, known as baleen whales, include humpbacks and grays. They feed by filtering tiny marine animals and small fish from the sea.

filtering – collecting tiny objects from the liquid they are floating in

What is baleen?

Instead of teeth, toothless whales have baleen – stiff, hairy sheets that hang in rows from their top jaws. Baleen traps food as water is filtered through it.

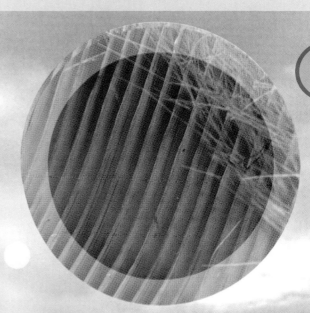

Big eaters

To eat enough, humpbacks gulp vast mouthfuls of water. Folds in their necks expand like a balloon to let in even more.

marine – from the sea

Clever hunters

All dolphins, porpoises and more than half of whale species have teeth. They eat fish and larger sea creatures. Sperm whales love to eat giant squid.

Fearless predators

The orca, often called the killer whale, is in fact a large dolphin. Its diet includes sealions and even other cetaceans.

predators – animals that hunt and eat other animals

Open wide

A dolphin's teeth are used for grabbing, not chewing. They swallow their prey whole.

Team work

Bottlenose dolphins often hunt together. They surround groups of fish, sometimes driving them onto land and coming halfway out of the water to grab them.

prey – animals eaten by other animals

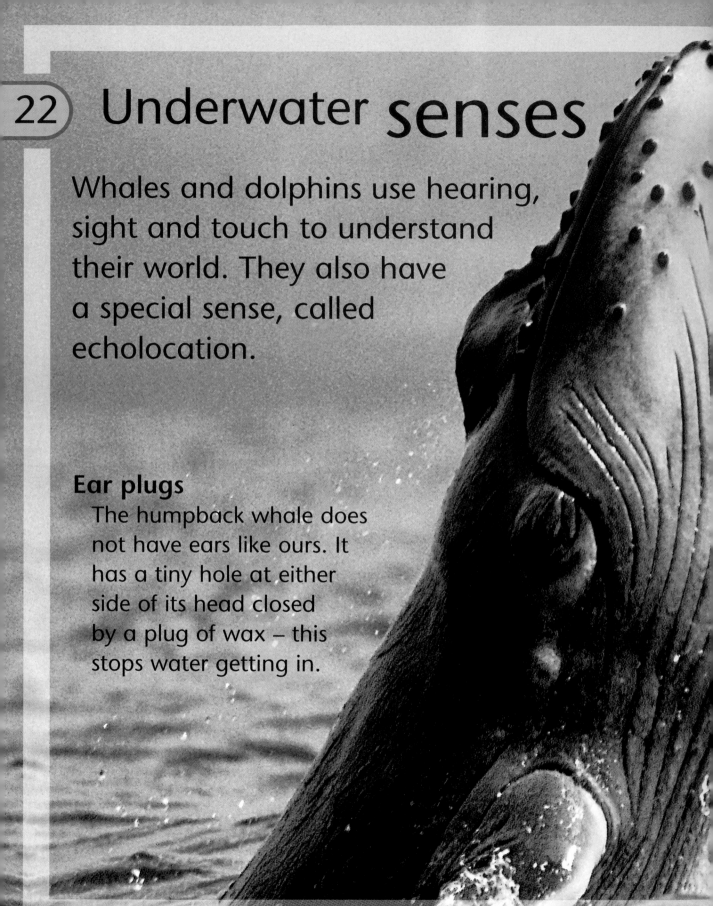

Underwater senses

Whales and dolphins use hearing, sight and touch to understand their world. They also have a special sense, called echolocation.

Ear plugs

The humpback whale does not have ears like ours. It has a tiny hole at either side of its head closed by a plug of wax – this stops water getting in.

wax – an oily material in the ear that protects it

What is echolocation?

Echolocation is used by dolphins to navigate and find prey. They make clicking noises that 'bounce', or echo, off an object, telling them where it is and what it is like.

Clear vision

They may have only small eyes, but most cetaceans see well. A thick, greasy liquid stops the eyes becoming sore in the salty water.

navigate – to find your way

Sea songs

All cetaceans use sounds to communicate. Baleen whales make low sounds, from loud grunts and squeals to bubbling noises. Dolphins whistle, squeak and click.

Noisy neighbours
Dolphins make different noises for different reasons. Jaw-clapping, opening and shutting their mouths, is a sign there may be a fight on the way.

communicate – *to send a message to another creature*

The latest tune

Male humpbacks sing patterns of notes and sounds that can last up to half an hour.

Brain power

Dolphins have large brains for the size of their bodies. They are fast learners and can even understand simple sentences.

brain – *the body part inside the head that is used to learn and think*

Playing with waves

From slapping their fins and tails on the surface to spinning in the air, cetaceans display all sorts of behaviour above the water as well as below.

High flyers

Dusky dolphins are among the most acrobatic of dolphins. They do breathtaking leaps and somersaults.

behaviour – how animals act

Who's there?
Orcas spyhop, sticking
their heads straight
up out of the water,
to spot penguins
    and seals on the ice.

A grand sight
When whales
launch themselves out
of the sea, it is called
breaching. Humpbacks have
been seen breaching 100
times, over and over again.

acrobatic – *doing movements that are difficult and skilful*

Moving home

Whales travel, or migrate, between cold seas in summer, where there is plenty of food, and warmer waters in winter, where they have their families.

Record holders

Humpbacks and grays make the longest journeys. They can swim up to 16,000 kilometres in a year.

North America

South America

breeding ground – where animals go to find a mate and have their young

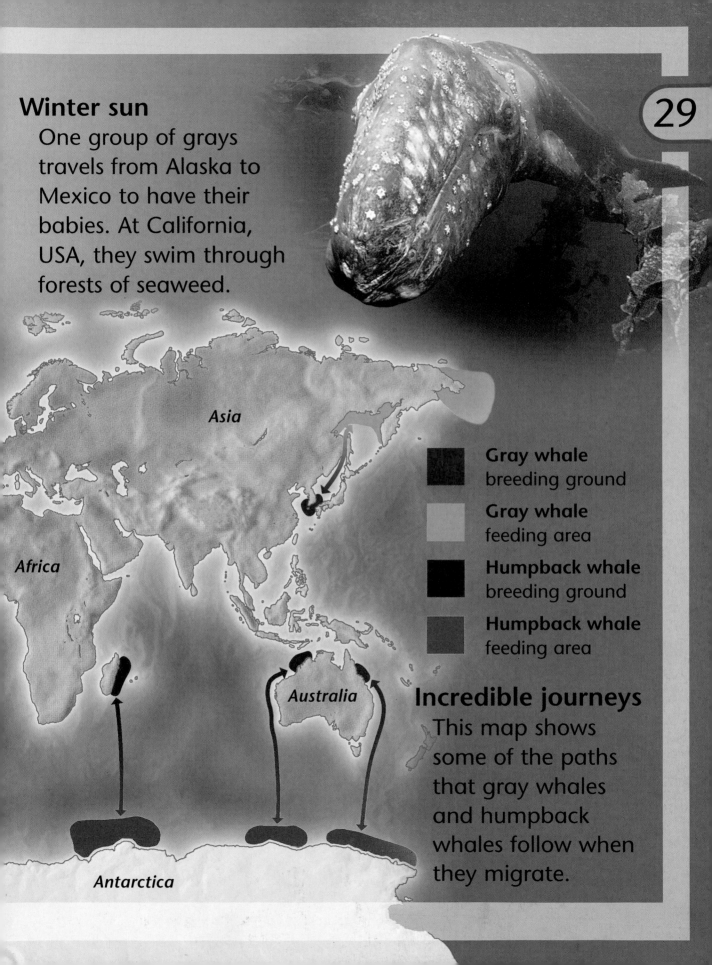

Winter sun

One group of grays travels from Alaska to Mexico to have their babies. At California, USA, they swim through forests of seaweed.

Asia

Africa

Gray whale breeding ground

Gray whale feeding area

Humpback whale breeding ground

Humpback whale feeding area

Australia

Incredible journeys

This map shows some of the paths that gray whales and humpback whales follow when they migrate.

Antarctica

New lives

Whale and dolphin babies swim as soon as they are born, but it takes many years until a calf is an adult.

Big babies

A humpback calf can measure a third of its mother's length when born! It will feed on her milk for the first 11 months.

pregnancy – the time when a baby grows inside its mother

Long pregnancy
Dolphins can be pregnant for more than a year. The actual birth, though, is quick and may be over in less than an hour.

Keeping close
Cetacean mothers stay close to their calves so they can protect them from predators.

Social animals

A group of cetaceans is known as a pod. Many pods are related, while others come together to feed or to protect young.

Family ties

All the members of an orca pod are related to one original mother or grandmother. Orcas usually stay with their family for life.

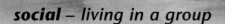

social – *living in a group*

Will to win

Adult males often travel together. Male narwhals clash tusks to decide which will have the right to mate with a female.

Touchy-feely

Atlantic spotted dolphins are often seen in pods of about ten. Animals in such groups will nudge each other in a friendly way.

related – part of the same family

Making friends

People have always seen dolphins as friendly creatures. Whales were once thought of as monsters, but today we want to protect them.

Watery friends

Swimming with dolphins has become popular with adults and children. Dolphins will even help people who are in trouble in the sea.

popular – liked by a lot of people

Ancient links

This painting of dolphins is on a wall at the Palace of Knossos on the Greek island of Crete. It is 3,500 years old.

Big books

There are many stories about giant whales. In the Bible, Jonah was swallowed by a whale – and survived.

Human dangers

Some things people do harm cetaceans. For a long time, whales have been hunted for their meat, baleen and blubber. Fishing nets and pollution are added dangers.

Whale rescue

Many dolphins and whales get caught and can die in fishing nets. This tangled-up sperm whale is being freed by a diver.

Under threat

The Yangtze river, China, is home to the baiji. This dolphin is endangered because the river is full of pollution.

endangered – in danger of dying out

Whaling ban

Whale hunting – known as whaling – has killed millions of cetaceans. Most countries have agreed to stop completely.

pollution – *harmful waste*

Growing knowledge

The more we discover about whales and dolphins, the more amazing we find they are. It is important to know as much as we can about them so that they can be better protected.

Getting to know them

Researchers can identify individual Risso's dolphins from the scars on their bodies. The pattern on each dolphin's body is different.

scars – marks left on the skin after cuts have healed

Satellite tagging

Cetaceans can now be followed from space! The tag on this beluga sends information to a satellite, which can then track where the beluga is.

satellite – a spacecraft that travels round and round the earth

Looking and learning

There are chances to watch whales, dolphins and porpoises in the wild throughout the world, from Ireland to the Caribbean and Canada to Australia.

Free to roam

Today, there are a few cetacean sanctuaries. It is hoped that in the future there will be more.

sanctuaries – safe places that are protected from damage by humans

Near the shore

Many species, especially of dolphins, come close to the coast. All you need to spot them is a pair of binoculars – and some patience.

Thrilling sight

Special boat tours can give a great view. Responsible tours do not crowd the animals and make sure they are not disturbed.

coast – where the land meets the sea

Dolphin mobile

Leaping high

Hang this mobile in your bedroom and you will have dolphins dancing before your eyes. Shiny paper makes them sparkle in the light.

You will need
- Pencil
- Tracing paper
- Thin cardboard
- Scissors
- Moulding dough
- Compass
- Foil/shiny paper
- Glue
- Ruler
- Ribbon
- Thick cardboard (30cm x 30cm)

dolphin template

Decorate each dolphin with foil or shiny paper

1

Trace the template and transfer the shape onto thin cardboard. Do this five times so you have five dolphins. Cut out the dolphins.

2

Place moulding dough under the top fin of each dolphin shape. Using a compass, make a hole in each fin as shown.

Draw a line from the bottom-left corner of the thick cardboard to the top-right corner using a ruler. Cut along the line to make two triangles and decorate them.

Cut a notch halfway down the peak of one triangle. Cut a notch halfway up from the bottom of the other triangle. Make holes at the ends of each triangle.

dolphin mobile

Slot the triangles together to form the hanger. Make a hole where the two triangles meet at the bottom and another at the top.

Use ribbon to attach each dolphin to the hanger and fasten the knots. Pull ribbon through the hole at the top of the hanger to make a loop. You can now hang up your mobile.

Whale bookmark

Intelligent creatures

Cetaceans are among the smartest animals. Make markers in the shape of sea mammals to keep your place in favourite books.

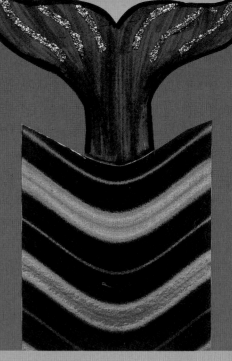

1

Measure a rectangle 6cm x 15cm. Draw a whale's tail at one short end of the shape. Draw waves where the tail meets the sea.

You will need
- Card
- Ruler
- Pencil
- Scissors
- Blue holographic paper
- Glue
- Felt-tip pens
- Glitter pens

2

Cut out the bookmark, being careful to cut around the shape of the whale's tail and around the top of the waves.

3

Glue blue holographic paper to both sides of the bookmark for the sea. Use felt-tip pens and glitter pens to colour in the tail.

Does it float?

Testing buoyancy

When you put different items in the water, some float on the surface and others sink to the bottom. Whales and dolphins need to come up for air, so they have to be bouyant enough not to sink straight down.

You will need
- Large clear bowl
- Water
- Apple
- Pebble
- Cork
- Ice cube

1

Think about the apple, pebble, cork and ice cube. Will they float or will they sink?

2 One by one, put each item into a bowl of water – were you right about which would float and which would sink?

Blue whale poster

Sea giants
Blue whales are the biggest animals on earth. They can reach 33 metres long, which is the size of a large swimming pool. This project will give you an idea of how large they are.

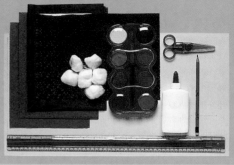

1

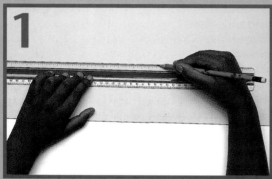

Using a ruler, measure and mark a 30cm space, then a 2cm space, an 8cm space, another 2cm space and, finally, a 6cm space.

You will need
- A1 card (66cm x 30cm)
- Ruler
- Pencil
- Paints
- Paintbrush
- Tissue paper: green, blue, red
- Glue
- Cotton wool
- Scissors
- Gold holographic paper

2

Draw a blue whale from tail to head in the 30cm space. Then draw an orca in the 8cm space and an elephant in the 6cm space.

3

Paint the blue whale, orca and elephant, copying the colours and markings shown on the final picture on the opposite page.

4

Decorate the picture with strips of tissue paper: green for land under the elephant and blue for the sea around the orca and whale.

5

Glue down cotton wool clouds. Then cut out a circle and 8 strips of gold holographic paper, and glue them down to make a sun.

To finish your picture, twist some red tissue paper and glue it down to create a border. Now you can see how large a blue whale is!

Index